OVERCOMING
SATANIC DEVICES

Bishop Nathaniel Wells Jr.

OVERCOMING SATANIC DEVICES

ReadersMagnet, LLC

Overcoming Satanic Devices
Copyright © 2020 by Bishop Nathaniel Wells Jr.

Published in the United States of America
ISBN Paperback: 978-1-952896-18-7
ISBN eBook: 978-1-952896-19-4

All rights reserved. No part of this publication may be reproduced, stored in a retrieval system or transmitted in any way by any means, electronic, mechanical, photocopy, recording or otherwise without the prior permission of the author except as provided by USA copyright law.

The opinions expressed by the author are not necessarily those of ReadersMagnet, LLC.

ReadersMagnet, LLC
10620 Treena Street, Suite 230 | San Diego, California, 92131 USA
1.619.354.2643 | www.readersmagnet.com

Book design copyright © 2020 by ReadersMagnet, LLC. All rights reserved.
Cover design by Ericka Obando
Interior design by Shemaryl Tampus

CONTENTS

Dedication ix
Introduction xi

Chapter 1. The Origin of Sin 1
Chapter 2. Satan in the Old Testament 5
Chapter 3. Devils in The Gospels 15
Chapter 4. Satan versus The Church and The Apostles . . . 24
Chapter 5. The Church of God in Christ's Position on
            Satanism 32
Chapter 6. The Power of the Tongue over Satan 42

The Final Summary 45

The Late Bishop Nathaniel Wells, Sr. & Mother Mildred Wells

Bishop L. H Ford

The Late Bishop J. O. Patterson

Dr. Clyde Young

DEDICATION

I AM DEDICATING THIS BOOK TO the following persons whom I feel have played such a vital part in my life and to whom I believe without their assistance I would not have achieved my goals.

Firstly, to my parents the Late Bishop Nathaniel Wells, Sr. and my mother, Mildred C. Wells, who set a pattern for me, by living a God Fearing life before me, being patient, loving, and understanding. For assisting and supporting Maryann and me in the early stages of our marriage: For building and establishing for me and the Saints in Western Michigan Jurisdiction a great image for which the Churches of God In Christ in this geographical area were built upon.

To a loving, faithful, and dedicated wife who has made her life's goal the rearing and nurturing of our five children and four grandchildren, and without question her quiet, but constant love, and support of her husband.

To the sainted memory of our fallen leader, the late Bishop J. O. Patterson, for the pattern and standard that he left to the Church of God In Christ.

To our Presiding Prelate, Bishop L. H. Ford, who saw in me things that no others had seen, and pulled me from the lower rung of the ladder to the highest class of leadership that the Church of God In Christ has to give, the office of Jurisdictional Bishop. Also for embracing me as a real son; by showing his

DEDICATION

concern through correction, words of encouragement, and wisdom. May God continue to preserve and keep our spiritual leader to continue to guide our great church to higher heights and deeper depths as we approach the 21st century.

To Dr. Clyde Young for his assistance and expertise in editing this book.

And last, but certainly not least, to God, for without him I would fail. To God be the Glory for the things he has done.

INTRODUCTION

The Church of God In Christ is a Pentecostal Church that embraces the Holiness doctrine. This being our denominational trait, we are strict believers in what the scripture says, particularly concerning Satan, demons, and evil. We use the Bible in our defense of what we believe about the unholy spirit opposing God, Christ, and the Church. This being the case we do not adhere to doctrine, theory, philosophy or teachings that are not interpreted in the light of biblical interpretations. We feel the scriptures give us the best account of who Satan is, where he came from, his demons and all the activities of evil perpetrated by him. The Bible is our book on all types of demonology and works of the devil in this world.

We, as members of the Church of God In Christ, do have a historical account of our founder, Bishop C. H. Mason, he was an Apostle and Evangelist who often used the words of the Angel, Michael, "Satan the Lord rebuke thee, Jude 1:9 and the promise to believers "In my name, they shall cast out devils." Mark 16:14.

The Bible and the Bible alone tells us that Satan, in his opposition to God and his Holy Angels in heaven, was overthrown, and a third of evil angels became earth's demons and in the earth's habitation cause those unholy activities displeasing to God, Christ, and the believers who make up the body of Christ called the "Church." We also embrace the biblical theory that all the evil activities in the Old Testament, the overthrowing of the world's empire, kingdoms and thrones destroyed where Satan reigned were those falling under God's almighty dominion. SATAN, and all the evil forces succumbing to scripture "The wicked shall be turned into hell and all nations that forget God," Psalm 9:17. Jesus said, "Hell is prepared for the devil and his angels (demons), Mt. 25:41. In the account of the devil being overcome and expelled from Heaven because of his evil pride and opposition to God, he was cast down to hell, Isa. 14:15 This evil warfare of SATAN against God and the church in this world does emanate from hell, but Jesus makes the promise of power to the church against all evil forces in Matthew 16:18 "Upon this rock, I will build my church and the gates of hell shall not prevail against it." I shall endeavor to point out in this book that scripture delves into all types of satanic activities of Satan in the twenty-first century. Since we shall not be ignorant of such devices in the future, we according to the prophetic proclamation of the Apostle Paul will be on guard to ever-increasing activities of Satan against the church and believers. His devices will entail the many faces of evil, the methods, and means at his disposal determined to reach his goal, to shame God, the church, and the believer in this Holy Ghost Age. But the scripture says "But they shall proceed no further for their folly shall be manifest unto all men, as theirs also was," Timothy 3:9. Men who are possessed by Satan and controlled by the forces of evil, do the biddings of Satan and suffer the consequence. We read in the scriptures, that Satan is styled as the "Prince of this world," whereby the Apostle John says to the believer "Greater is He that is in you than he that is in the world," I John 4:4. Though the many forces of evil in this, the twentieth century, there are many characterized as fortune-telling, witchcraft, sorcery, divination, and secret orders, all are classified in the true church as satanic devices. Even in this highly specialized, technological world, Satan has devices in evil inventions spoken of in II Timothy 3:1-7, all evils therein defined are perpetrated by Satan, himself, seducing men of this age, even as Eve was deceived by the serpent: The tempter, seducer and the "Accuser of the brethren" still wages war against God, Christ, and His Church. In this book, I shall uncover many devices of Satan and his "Modus Apperendus" or method of operation against saints and believers. I hope to help fortify, educate, and protect every believer so he/she won't fall victim to the temptations of Satan in this era of the church.

CHAPTER 1

THE ORIGIN OF SIN

"Who Is Satan?" "Where did he come from?" The Revelation given to the Prophet Isaiah in chapter 14 verse 12-19 speaks of Satan's presumption that he had spoken in his heart (mind) concerning his intended elevation in heaven. "For thine, hast said in thine heart, I will ascend into heaven." This was the origin of evil spoken about one called "Lucifer," Son of the Morning. In ancient Jewish history, some writers would say it was Canaanite myths - that this exalted angel was called "Day Star" or "Lightgiver," and "Son of the Dawn." But we in Christian literature believe that this same "Lucifer" was Satan or the devil, the one who would challenge God by thinking evil thoughts, "I will ascend above the heights of the clouds I WILL BE LIKE THE HIGHEST." The modern writers of Christian literature have much to ponder as they give to us the cause and the consequences of evil, how Satan or so-called "Lucifer," Son of the morning, an Arch Angel, in heaven was defeated, dethroned and cast from his lofty position.

Let's examine the truth written concerning this allegory

or Jewish myth, we call Isaiah's revelation about Satan and the origin of evil.

First, the Judgement of Pride "yet thou shalt be brought down to the pits of Hell, to the sides of the pit, Isaiah 14:15.

Second, the failure of success, when it's not calculated with the integrity of righteousness "What shall it profit a man, if he gains the whole world, and lose his soul, his friends, his faith, his God," said Jesus, Luke 9:25

Third, the final consequence of evil desires and ungodly achievements. "Lucifer was cast out," "How art thou fallen from heaven?" The Book of Revelation chapter 12 verse 7 puts the pieces together from chapter 14 of the Prophet Isaiah, "Lucifer was cast down because there was war in heaven, Michael and his angels, fought against the dragon," Rev. 12:7. The name given to Lucifer is now changed to "Dragon" in the book of Revelation of Jesus Christ. "And the great dragon was cast out, the old serpent, called the devil. The Apocalypse tells of the devil's fate, and the tail (authority) drew a third of heaven with him and the stars were cast down to earth." Connecting these two passages of scripture gives us the pieces of the missing part of Satan's fate and the origin of evil. Satan being cast out of heaven, cast into the earth. The revelations of Jesus Christ to the church tells us of his awful, hateful, revengeful nets to mankind after being evicted and expelled from his lofty heights of heaven. The Bible says "Woe unto the earth and the sea (masses of people) because the devil is come down, having great fury) because he knoweth that he hath but a short time," Rev. 12:12,13. The devil is a defeated foe, he is an angry foe, he is a revengeful foe. Later in the chapter, it tells of his evil attack upon the church which was styled as the "woman in the wilderness," Rev. 12:13.

Examine again Satan's origin of evil in heaven, the presumptuous evil thoughts, the evil pride, the desire to possess the position that belongs to God Almighty, and God Almighty alone.

The Apostle Paul warns believers of the satanic strongholds. Let's hear what the Apostle Paul warns saints about concerning evil thoughts that become strongholds of the mind. The same strongholds that dethroned Satan, who was called "Son of the Morning." "Cast down imaginations, and every high thing that exalteth itself against the knowledge of God and bringing into captivity every thought to the obedience of Christ, II Cor. 10:5." The Living Bible puts it in these terms "The weapons of righteousness can break down every proud argument against God." It can capture the rebel thoughts and bring them back into the desire to be obedient to Christ. Therefore, we conclude that Satan or the devil in heaven called "Shining One" or the "Enlightened One" did not control the evil thoughts of being like the highest. This was the beginning of evil, the beginning of right versus wrong, sin versus righteousness, the devil verses God and His Son, Jesus Christ. The Hebrew root of the word Satan means, "The opposed One" it speaks of that name as one who plays the part of the adversary in general and especially in the court of law. In the Greek he is called, "Diabolus," the hated one, the one of hostility, or hatred. In the Old Testament, he is referred to as a superhuman being "That do exercise evil" and the Apostle Paul in Ephesians 6 says, "We wrestle not against flesh and blood:" it's spiritual warfare against a spiritual giant. In the old testament, he is called "Satan the Archdemon and direct antithesis of Yahweh." In all of Jewish religious history from the Old Testament to the New Testament of the gospels, Satan is viewed as one who sows discord and violence among men. He is the author of Lasciviousness, evil thoughts, and evil-mindedness; he conspired against Joseph and all the patriarchs, the cause of sickness, controller of evil men, flying through the air on his failed mission. All human tribulation is due to the master-violence, the obstructor of good men, of God, and lastly, he is depicted in Jewish allegory as commanding his rival hosts in fatal combat toward God, tempting Eve to cause Adam to sin. He is the deceiver is depicted in Jewish allegory as one condescending to the servant in order to do evil against mankind. He eventually succumbs to his doom and those who he beguiled.

In the Hebrew definition of Satan, it also renders the word, destructive angel, "to destroy you" these were common synonyms to the word SATAN. We do accept the "Old and New Testament styling him as the "Father of Lies" and in opposition to the Holy Spirit, which is the spirit of truth. Even in the New Testament the word Satan is termed as accuser, persecutor, and one ruling over the regions of "Darkness." This is also spoken of by Paul, who was of the Rabbinical school, calling Satan the "Ruler of Darkness." Thus, we have concluded that throughout the ages of Bible history, Satan, or the Devil is the author of sin, evil, and transgression.

CHAPTER 2

SATAN IN THE OLD TESTAMENT

W E MUST APPROACH SATAN AND Demon activities in the Old Testament with the view that before God appeared to Abraham in Ur of the Chaldeans, the people who were engrossed in "religious beliefs" of which most of it was paganism and idol worship. Their paganism had to do with the belief of the unknown spirits, the worship of nature and superstition, out of which grew witchcraft, sorcery and all sorts of religious practices that were devil oriented and satanically controlled. The Apostle Paul on Mars Hill, when confronted with the Greek's complete maze of idols to worship, told them, "I perceive that in all things you too are superstitious," Acts 17:22. The root of the words religious and superstitious are the same. Its base interpretation and belief have to do with the fear and worship of the unknown. The Greeks were wise, intellectual and the most learned people of their day, but not knowing the real and true God, they were enslaved by religious superstitions and idols which they worshipped.

The Apostle Paul told them the time of this ignorance did God winked (or overlook because of his mercy) but now have commanded men everywhere to repent. Therefore, before the times of both Abraham and Moses, there were satanic activities shrouded in these religious and superstitious practices, which in most cases were ancient idol worship.

Let's take a look at the Patriarch Abraham and his family background in Haran. Abram was born in Haran of Mesopotamia and his people in that area worshipped the moon god. The people of "Ur" called "Chaldeans" were near ancient Babylon and they migrated into Southern Mesopotamia, where people were skilled in astrology, fortune-telling, dream interpretation, and other types of pseudo-sciences. The name "Chaldeans" came to mean Astrologers, sooth-sayers, etc. This location of the Chaldeans is northwest of the present Persian Gulf, near the junction of the River Euphrates. Abram was born right in the cross-roads of these cultures that were deep in Paganism, idol worship, and nature worshippers such as the "Moon Gods of Ur." For God to reveal himself fully to Abram as the true and only God; God called him out of this environment that his father and other relatives had lived in for centuries. We can see the plan of Satan, which was to conquer all those regions with the demonic spell of witchcraft, sorcery, and other forms of Paganistic religions. It is written in the Book of the Rabbis a story of Jewish mythology concerning how God revealed himself to Abram as the true and living God: Abram's father, Terah was an idol maker and had idols of all sizes in his shop. One day Terah had to leave the shop and left young Abram to oversee the shop until he returned. Abram accidentally broke one of the small idols and was fearful for his life, but nothing happened, so the curious youngster purposely broke a second, and a third idol, and so on until all the idols were broken and there was a mess in the shop: Upon his father's return, and saw all the broken idols, he questioned young Abram, "What happened while I was gone?" Abram responded, "The idols became angry and begin to fight among themselves." Terah told young Abram "you are not telling me the truth; the idols have no life." It was at that time that young Abram knew that the idols were helpless, thus false. God then spoke to him and said, "leave this country, your father's house, and your kindred and go to a land that I will show thee," Genesis 12:1. Abram obeyed God and stepped out on faith, God blessed him with gold, silver, and cattle, Genesis 13:1.

How real and how effective was pagan religion under the domination of Satan. Let's look at Moses when he stood before Pharaoh when he brought his rod of miracles to the King's Court. God knew that Egypt, like all of the countries, nations, and regions, were engrossed in the Pagan religion. He told Moses to cast down his rod before Pharaoh and it would turn into a serpent, but Pharaoh called on the ancient enchanters that were always ready in the King's Court. The magicians, wise men, and soothsayers did as Moses did, their rods also became serpents (snakes). How real then is magic? How real is demonism or Satanism? How real is the evil spirit world? The magicians in Pharaoh's court duplicated Moses' magic rods turning them to live serpents. We must remember what Jesus says about the Devil's crafts, which are signs and wonders. Matt. 24:24 *"For there shall arise false Christ and false prophets, and shall show great signs and wonders."*

Therefore, we must conclude, that Voodoo, witchcraft, curses, magic, and the entire evil spirit world does have real signs and real wonders such as those magicians showed Moses and Aaron. Moses' serpent and Aaron ate or consumed those of the Magicians in Pharaoh's court, always showing and demonstrating that God is greater and supreme. This confirms the declaration of the Apostle John asserted to the church "Greater is He that is in you than he that is in the world," I John 4:4. All through the

Old Testament the works of Satan in the methods and means of magic, witchcraft, and sorcery had been prevalent, but God did not want his people to be in bondage to religious superstition, and that's why Abraham and Moses were called and prepared by God to go out, to be separate, to be different from their ancestor's environment. God appeared to Abram with the proclamation "I am the Almighty God, walk before me and be perfect," Genesis 17:1. God was telling Abram what would be revealed to him later, that there were no other living gods but Him. Those that appeared as gods were demons, false spirits, and the works of Satan. Israel was forbidden to be involved with "familiar spirits" and was by covenant asked to put to death any woman practicing witchcraft: "Suffer not a witch to live," Ex. 22:18, was one of the covenant commandments in the Israelite camp. In the book of Job, chapter one, it shows in almost story form, Satan appearing with Job before God. There the scripture gives us the picture of Satan having a conversation with God concerning Job. The devil inflicts trouble, sickness, and turmoil upon Job by the permission of God. Job finally triumphs in the end.

In the Book of the Prophets, Isaiah speaks of the practice of demonic activity among backsliding Israel when in the Book of Prophecy of Isaiah in the 2nd chapter, verse 6, they are rebuked, "The Lord has rejected you because you welcome foreigners from the East who practice magic and communicated with evil spirits as do the Philistines," (Living Bible). All these practices of demons came under the title of "Divination" from which the modern religious world gets the word divine. This connotation does not always have to refer to True Godliness, but also satanism and Satan worship. Isaiah Chapter 14, verse 13, rebukes Israel for their multitude of false advisers such as the astrologers, the stargazers, the prognosticators (monthly horoscopes), fortune tellers, etc. The prophet Isaiah assures them that the enchantments and sorceries will not profit them in the days of calamities. It also was interpreted that satanic powers in the air spoken of by Daniel in chapter 10:13, when the Angel Michael told the prophet that his prayer of 21 days was heard but the "The Prince of the Kingdom of Persia withstood me." This was an indication of satanic resistance. Satan may hinder, but never stop the progress of the righteous. Thus we have proved that in the Old Testament, after creation and the fall of man, Satanism and demon activity had plagued the entire world making all its subjects' servants of false religion, witchcraft, sorcery and idol worshipping. Thank God for the call of Abraham, because it was the beginning of man's worship of the true and living God, rather than some unknown god shrouded in fear and mystery of superstition. This true revelation to Abraham concerning the true and real God, not a false God, was given to the Jews and later to the Christians. Our faith, which has nothing to do with superstitious religion which is Satan controlled, but rather a faith built upon the factual historical record of the birth, life, death, and resurrection of Jesus Christ, as expressed by Jesus to Peter, "Upon this rock, I will build my church and the very gates of hell shall not prevail against it." Matt. 16:18(b). The church is built not on Peter or his personality, but the confession of Peter, "Thou art the Christ, the Son of the Living God!" Matt. 16:16

THE WITCH AT ENDOR

(I Samuel 28:7-20)

Here we have in the Old Testament a real eerie, horror, story of the modern Halloween type, suitable for one of Hollywood's weird productions of the "World Beyond." This story, this account, is not in some horror novel, it's not the creation of some playwright's imagination, but rather it is from the Holy Book, the Bible, it's not fictitious, it's real, and its fact. It shows the reality of demonic activity in witchcraft, sorcery and in this case, necromancy and black arts (communication with the dead).

The Bible does not cover-up nor does it smooth over strange accounts in the scripture, but is very vivid and candid, leaving us in many instances to interpret as we see, with our theological minds making exegesis according to scripture references, conformations, and documentations.

Let's take a close look at the persons and events in this bazaar, strange, but a true event in the Old Testament. In this story, disposed King Saul was contending for some supernatural word or message concerning the upcoming battle with the Philistine Army. The dejected and rejected Saul, not surrendering to his God-given successor, David, who slew Goliath, would not be given a message by God, neither by dreams or by the Prophet. But King Saul was determined not to be outdone so he resorted to having the future told him by a medium or a witch, called a woman with a "familiar spirit." Though he, according to the Law of Moses, had all those who practiced such witchcraft, black arts, or in this necromancy killed. But in desperation, he seeks out this woman that the devil had given the power to practice the art of "calling up the dead." The witch at Endor, knew that witchcraft was forbidden in Israel, and that those servants who found her could also turn her in to have her meet the fate of capital punishment, but like all other evils in the city that are illegal, you can find someone practicing it. Saul assured the woman of her safety and proceeded to make his ungodly request "Bring me up, Samuel." She was terrified when she recognized that it was the king himself seeking this demonstration of the medium of black arts. Bring up from the grave the dead prophet?

What a mysterious request, how strange and eerie. Perhaps the witch did go into her trance and chant, telling Saul what she saw. (I saw gods ascending out of the earth) or being interpreted by commentary "I see one like a god," or "one in a supernatural form." The woman described what she saw, and it was identified by Saul as the Prophet Samuel. Even though Israel believed in life after death, which is evident in the writings of Job, and the Psalms, etc. We too according to the scriptures heard Jesus say "God is not the God of the dead, but of the living," Matt. 22:32. Also, Jesus talked with Moses and Elijah in the mountains (Matt. 17:3), thus making it scripturally sound that departed persons can come back and appear when God permits. The description of Samuel by the witch, the voice, and prophecy of doom by the dead prophet are all recorded in this Old Testament account of demonic activity concerning a king who was doomed by God, and who heard his fate spoken by the resurrected Samuel, who had no news other than what Saul's guilty conscience was already telling him since he was rejected by God.

DO THE DEAD COMMUNICATE WITH THE LIVING?

In the case of Saul and Samuel, where it was God's will to turn him over to the supernatural workings of demons, using this horrified witch, is not the ordinary. Israel was forbidden to delve into wizardry, sorcery, or the black arts of the mediums, which were the gods of Egypt, Persia Babylonia, and other heathen pagan kingdoms. The New Testament is the modern Christian's evidence that all kinds of witchcraft, mediums, soothsayers, and sorcerers are all of the devils. The astrologers and moon gazers are all the work of Satan, who promotes idolatry, superstitions and the worship of Satan. According to Jesus' message regarding the death of Lazarus and the rich man, who was in torment, asked for communication with his living brothers, but was told that there was a "Great Gulf" that separates the living from the dead, (Luke 16:26). This great schism separating the living from the dead remains intact today, but often we hear of those who have gone to mediums and practice necromancy seeking to get messages from the departed dead. As Christians, we don't believe the devil has the power to arouse the dead, and allow them to communicate with the living. Devils cannot do what God forbids, but if God desires the departed to reappear in some form as he did when Jesus talked to Elijah and Moses at the Transfiguration. Also, dead saints were seen walking through Jerusalem after the resurrection (Matt. 27:25), so there are instances and incidents where God of Jesus commands or permits the dead to communicate with the living. Thus, witches controlled by devils could hardly call from the dead departed love ones.

"OVERCOMING SATANIC DEVICES"

Old Testament Summary

In the Old Testament era and times, we can see the hand of Satan in his effort to bring the whole world under the domination of false religion. The many faces of the satanically controlled religions were those of idolatry, nature, deity worship, witchcraft, sorcery, wizardry, the black arts, mediums, (fortune-telling, etc.) and most of all, polytheism (the belief in many and multiple gods). Abraham was called in the Mesopotamian area about the time of these religious and superstitious practices. The

Apostle Paul on Mar Hill rebuked the Athenians Greeks who were religious (Superstitious) idol worshippers, saying to them, "The time of this ignorance did God wink, or better translated in the modern Bible, God tolerated man's past ignorance about those things, but now commands everyone to put away idols and worship the true God," Acts 17:30. God's revelation to the Patriarch Abraham was, "I am the Almighty God" which was later to be revealed to all of the patriarchs, that He alone was the only God, that created heaven, earth, all nature, and all mankind. During the years when Israel was in Egypt, they were taught and instructed in the Egyptian polytheistic gods that manifested themselves in many forms of idols. They were surrounded by many pagan tribes, even when they were delivered from Egypt that took Israel as having a god that delivered them, a god that many heathens around Israel did not accept as the God of the whole universe.

Israel was constantly reminded of the laws of Moses "Hear 0 Israel the Lord thy God is one Lord," Deut. 6:4. This early revelation to Israel in the law was not meant to disprove the Trinity but was emphatically stated to remind Israel that this one and only God, is not like the Egyptian, Babylonian, nor Persian belief that there are many and other gods. The later revelation in scripture would prove that the god "Elohim" which in Hebrew was the plural god of majesty from which the Christian literature would arrive at the Trinity: Father, Son, and Holy Ghost. In the whole Pagan and heathen world, Satan had implanted in the mind of men who feared the wrath of gods, that there were many gods having power over men and the universe, but God through the revelation given to Abraham revealed to his generation that God and God only controlled the universe inhabited by man. The Prophet Elijah on Mount Carmel mocked the god, Baa, who was not able to send the fire, nor cause rain. Elijah won the victory turning Israel back to God. after Ahab's idolatrous wife Jezebel caused Israel to be under the domination of Baal.

Abraham later found out that God Jehovah was not "transcendent," but it was the gods of Babylon and Persia that were limited because they had no life, but God was a God that communicated, a God that was faithful, true, merciful, and a loving God. But Satan in his superstitious religious type was a distorted being, destructible and unpredictable in his actions to man.

In the Book of Romans, the Apostle Paul explains in chapter one, how man came under the domination of Satan's idolatry "who changed the truth of God into a lie and worshipped and served the creature more than the creator, who is blessed forever, Amen."

Furthermore, Paul in his epistle to the Corinthians talks about controlling those ungodly thoughts that become "strongholds in the minds of men who profess to be wise and become fools. We should pull down any of those imaginations that exalts itself against the knowledge of God, and bring into captivity to the obedience of Christ. We finally say concerning religion and Satan's activities in Old Testament times he had captured the whole world in his false religion of the many gods, the many deities, and forms of false religious beliefs before God revealed himself to Abraham as the one and only true God of the universe.

CHAPTER 3

DEVILS IN THE GOSPELS

Demonic activities in the New Testament has its classic examples as to how Jesus Christ, the Son of God dealt with all demonic activities. The word demon or demons is not in the scripture but rather its roots come from the Latin word, "Daemon" and in Greek "Daeimon." This reference to the devil in the Greek is the word "Daeirnon," this word does refer to a deity or spirit that is invisible, incorporeal (can be joined to combine with another). This deity causes all types of evil activities. In the scriptures, they are referred to as the angels who lost their estate, II Peter 2:4, Jude 1:6. Jesus in the New Testament calls the devil, an unclean spirit and refers to him as "Thief" in John 10:10 and parables, "The Wolf" and "The Enemy." Jesus also knew that Satan with his incorporeal power could combine with certain human personalities such as "King Herod" whom Jesus called a "Fox," Luke 13:32. By far and large the account of satanic activity in the New Testament showing how devils reacted as they met Jesus the Son of God. When they met him, He was their master, He tormented them, He overcame them, He gave them orders, He rebuked them and cast them out of humans. As the writer,

Luke wrote in the Book of Acts, Chapter 10 verse 38 "How God anointed Jesus of Nazareth with the Holy Ghost and with power, who went about doing good, healing all oppressed of the devil for God was with Him." This conclusive statement about Jesus, his ministry, and how he overcame Satan shows us that Jesus moved among people doing good, and when the devil, the oppressor, of humankind was present he had the power to overcome him.

JESUS MEETS DEVILS

In the gospel of Matthew, Chapter 4, Jesus meets the devil after his wilderness experience and Satan attempts to deceive him, asking that Jesus, the Son of God, would bow down and worship him. Jesus moves through those times in the New Testament record, defeating demons that were causing men to be dumb, blind or afflicted with certain ailments, such as leprosy, palsy, and certain spiritual vexations. In Matthew 15:22-28, Jesus heals the Canaanite woman's daughter that was vexed with a devil, and the woman shows courageous faith and persisted even when called "Dogs" receiving her request.

Matthew 17:18 a man had a son who was a "Lunatic" in Greek the word is "Selania" or one that is "moonstruck," who wobbles or totters when walking. This type of affliction would be like unto our palsy today. This condition was agitated by a devil, which Jesus rebuked and healed. The unclean spirit cried out to Jesus in torment "Let us alone, what have we to do with thee, Jesus of Nazareth? Art thou come to destroy us?" Jesus would not let these foul spirits give glory to Him, He rebuked them and cast them out. "Hold thy peace," he commanded them. Onlookers were astonished at his power to control demons and they often said "What kind of man is this, for with authority and power he commandeth unclean spirits and they come out. Jesus was the "Exorcist" to devils, that is he had the power to free men from the evil spirits that caused ailments, affliction and other types of satanic oppressions. In Mark 3:15, Jesus ordained the twelve disciples and gave them the power to cast out devils. They all had the power of exorcism "except Judas" whom Jesus said was a devil, John 6:70.

JESUS AND BEELZEBUB

In the Gospels of Mark and Luke, we have the account of the Pharisees and hypocrites accusing Jesus of using his "Exorcist Power" to cast out devils using another devil, Beelzebub. Beelzebub in the Old Testament was "God of the Flies" but is the "Prince of Devils" in the New Testament, Matt. 12:24. The Jews had long believed that "Beelzebub was described having supreme authority among spirits. They would say of Jesus that Beelzebub had lesser demons at Jesus' command to cast out other devils by the authority of Beelzebub. Jesus argued the point that Beelzebub could not give him the power to cast out devils because that would divide the kingdom of the devils. Jesus said, "I cast out devils by the power of God and if Satan cast out Satan, he is divided against himself. How can his kingdom stand? Furthermore, Jesus acknowledged to the Pharisees, "But if I cast out devils by the Spirit of God, then the Kingdom of God has come unto you." The Apostle Paul further tells how the evil kingdom operates in this world under the domination of Satan in Ephesian 6:12, he states that Satan operates his principality, his power of evil and rulers of darkness and spiritual wickedness in high places.

JESUS MEETS LEGION "AEGEW"

In the Gospels of Matthew and Luke, Jesus meets those possessed of the Devil, those living among the tombs, naked, fierce, crying in torment, having superhuman strength even to the breaking of iron chain. On the occasion of meeting the man of God, A-renes, near Galilee, Jesus talks to the possessed with devils, the Devil speaking out of the man responded to the question asked by Jesus, "What is thy name?" The spokesman for the possessed said, "Legion" A legion according to the Roman world during this time was 6,826 men in a military body. This being the case, that's over 6,000 incorporate spiritual personalities inhabiting one body. This would present to modern Psychiatric phenomena, a unique situation of one with an extreme condition of a schizophrenic psychopath, having these separate tormenting demons, giving men the multiple frustrations in one human body. The tormented soul was set free by Jesus with just words, "Come out of him," "Go." They asked permission to enter feeding swine, for which they made their haste after the "Exorcism." The swine, being greatly disturbed stamped down the hillside and drowned in the lake below. This account in the New Testament Gospels gives us more evidence that Jesus, on many occasions met devils doing all sorts of evil, causing all sorts of illnesses, ailments, and afflictions that were conquered by him.

In the case of mental disorders and mental illness, the Apostle Paul admonishes the church to be on guard for it. In I Thess. 5:14, he asked the saints to "Comfort the feeble-minded, knowing that Satan takes advantage of the feeble minds just as he does feeble bodies and works havoc where he can."

THE FUTILITY FOR SELF-REFORMATION

In the gospel Jesus presents the story, message, or parable narrated in Matthew 12:43, he speaks of the unclean spirit departing. He does not say on what occasion, as to whether he was cast out by exorcism or whether he was expelled by the man's imagination of human resistance. The Apostle James speaks of believers "resisting the devil," thereby causing him to flee. We would like to think in the terms of the exegesis of this text, that Jesus was telling of the strong human will to rid one's self of satanic evils, but being without God, unable to attain those pure goals. Satan himself will leave for a season and come back to his old habitation, finding it clean, but not protected, returning to that house to overpower it with seven devils worst then himself and to destroy that person. Jesus talks about the power of his Word, his kingdom, and the saving grace that will enable human personalities to withstand the onslaught of Satan. The Apostle Paul tells the saints "Know ye not that your body is the temple of the Holy Ghost." Jesus was narrating this story about the futility of self-reformation to warn the world, you are no match for Satan, but I am. If you have Christ in your life, you have power over demons. In the Gospel we have Jesus warning Simon, his chief Apostle, "Simon, Simon, Satan desires to have you, that he may sift you like wheat, but I prayed for you and when thou art converted, strengthen thy brethren." Luke 22:3.

MY NAME IS LEGION
"For We Are Many"

According to scriptures both in the Old Testament prophecy of Isaiah 14 and in the New Testament, of the Revelation of Jesus

Christ, Chapter 12, one-third of heaven's forces became subject to "Lucifer," called the "Old Dragon" and the "Devil," which was cast out of heaven. The Devil with his evil angels lost the war and their heavenly habitation. They were cast out of heaven and came down to planet earth. This happened possibly eons of years before the creation of man and we see him manifested in the serpent in the Garden of Eden in Genesis, Chapter 3. As far as the number of fallen angels cast to the earth, they were probably in the millions, if not billions. They not being able to procreate (give birth) were still in large numbers in their new habitation, the planet earth. In Revelation 12:12, these angelic evil beings were full of wrath toward God and became known as the "accusers of the brethren" or those evil beings, who do not like the presence of God. They will appear before God to accuse the people of God. These dethroned beings (Spiritual) became the evil forces of the world, the evil principality, and workers of the power of darkness and wickedness upon mankind. One-third of the angels under God's authority are the protectors of the good in the earth and heaven. Just as the occasion in II Kings 6:16,17, the Prophet Elisha prayed that God would open the eyes of the young prophet who could only see the surrounding Syrian Army and could not see the greater, more powerful angelic army surrounding them: Elisha said, "There are more than be with us than they that be with them." Therefore, there are far more good angels on the side of the righteous than there are evil angels against us," Psalm 34:7.

    The devil appeared to Jesus in the wilderness of Temptation in Matthew 4:4-10, Satan propositioned Jesus THAT HE (Satan) had possession, of souls of men in kingdoms, that he would give to Jesus, the Son of God if he would "Bow down and worship him." The temptations of Jesus by the devil, show that the many forces in the earth are evil bargainers for men's souls, "But what shall a man give in exchange for his soul?" Mark 8:37.

There are many types, forms, expressions and religions of Satan. The many faces of Satan are the mediums, witchcraft, sorcerers, voodoo, etc. The many types of satanic expressions in the earth are horoscopes, magic prognosticators, fortune telling, séances, and the practices of witches, and witch-doctors. In the lands where the true revelation of God and Jesus Christ have not been preached, Satan has already introduced some types of superstitious religious forms of worship, such as cults, and satanic practices. In the case of the demonic man in the tomb, where the devil spoke out of him at the request of Jesus to state their name. Their reply was Legion because they were many demons in one person and different devils in the one personality. This Legion which according to a Roman military body or unit numbers over 6,000. They were the many forms, types, and manifestation in the one man, tormenting the one human being. They being many could possess a human personality causing many disturbances, disruption, and human harm. These same demonic beings asked permission to enter the swine since Jesus was casting them out of the young man. They were given the permission to "go" or to leave the man, did enter the herd of swine. These contended with the embodiment of devils and ran violently down a slope into the sea and were drowned.

WE ARE MANY

There were many demons, many devils, and there were many evil personalities, evil poison indecent, and corrupt spirits. The many demons caused damage to society and in the communities of humanity. There are many types of demons, devils, all forms of affliction, disease, sickness, and indecency in the world. They bring fear, unsafe practice, war, division, and all forms of social evil in the country and the societies of this world. This host of hell, these demons of destruction that perpetrate evil, and these spirits of degeneracy and devilish activities that possess humankind, were created for the glory of God, yet they interfere, causing sin and compelling men to do those things against the will of God. This ultimately draws souls to eternal damnation prepared for the Devil and his angels. Though the devil has many sinful operations, many evil inventions, and corrupt practices, they can be defeated and overcome. Jesus gave the Apostles power to "Cast out Devils." "Behold, I give unto you power to tread on serpents and scorpions and over all the power of the enemy and nothing shall by any means hurt you," Luke 10:19. The devil and the demons are many, though they have many unhealthy, unholy operations for bad and evil, they can be brought down from their lofty heights and subdued in this world by the righteous, who do so in the name of Jesus Christ, the Son of the Living God.

THE SUMMARY

We can readily see in the New Testament that Jesus exposes us to the power and the failures of Satan to defeat the Kingdom of God. He encounters satanic activity all along his journey, in Palestine and Judea. He met devils in every walk of life, afflicting people, causing sickness, ailments, and disease. Jesus was in full command, always the victor, always overcoming, and always triumphing over Satan and demons who cried out when they saw him, giving him the right of way because he was the Son of God. Jesus would not allow them to identify him nor give him distinction. He rebuked them and commanded them to "Hold their peace." Jesus also made other references to Satan as the evil one, making him responsible for sowing tares among the wheat, and that Satan was the "Thief," the destroyer, and the tormentor of mankind. In all of the gospels, Jesus becomes the conquering King, the Lord of Lords, even over the grave, death, and hell, proclaiming at the resurrection, "I have all power both in heaven and in the earth."

CHAPTER 4

SATAN VERSUS THE CHURCH AND THE APOSTLES

Though Jesus gave the Apostles power over satanic activities as mentioned in Luke 10, Satan was busy opposing the saints and the Apostles in the early church. We shall trace his activities and his subsequent defeat. In the Acts of the Apostles, chapter 5, when Annias and Sapphira, conspired to hold back money on a property that was sold. This was money the Apostles could use to care for the needs of the saints that did not have. Annias and Sapphira conspired together to say this was the total amount that the piece of land sold for, and laid the money at the Apostles feet. The Apostle Peter had been given by the Holy Ghost the real situation concerning the matter, how they sold possession of their land and kept back part of the price, he said to them "Why hath Satan filled thine heart to lie to the Holy Ghost?"

In both the gospel of Luke, Chapter 22 and John 13:27, the scriptures tell of Satan entering the heart of Judas. This gives us evidence of satanic control and satanic possession. Satan can spiritually penetrate the mind and intents of the human will. For Satan to take over a person's mind, he has to be able to enter and occupy the thoughts of the human mind. Though man has the power to withstand satanic suggestions and to refuse his powers, Satan will take advantage of the human will as he did in the case of Annias and his wife Sapphira. Also, when Simon, the follower of the Apostles in Acts, Chapter 8, who asked the unholy proposition, "Give me also this power that whomsoever I lay hands on may receive the Holy Ghost." He saw that the Apostles laid hands on the believers and they received the Holy Ghost, however, the Apostles refused his money when he wanted to buy this gift from them. Peter rebuked him and said, "Thy money perish with thee because they thought that the gift of God may be purchased with money." With this being thought and suggestion of Satan, the Apostle Peter said, " I perceive that thou art in the gall of bitterness and the bond of iniquity." Acts 8:18-23.

THE APOSTLES MEET WITH SATANIC ACTIVITIES

In the Book of Acts, Chapter 16, we see a case of a young woman that was demon-possessed. She was as described by scripture a damsel possessed with a spirit of divination. She was used by a master or a man who exploited her gift of soothsaying. This gift by Satan was that of "fore-telling" or fortune-telling. The damsel brought in money to her master by this evil practice and met the Apostles following them daily, crying out **"These men are the servants of the highest God, which shew unto us the way of Salvation."** But after many days of this praise by the satanic spirit in the damsel, the Apostle Paul perceived that the evil spirit was using the damsel and being annoyed by the evil spirit rebuked the foul spirit within the woman. "I command thee in the name of Jesus Christ to come out of her." Her masters or those who exploited her, lost their financial gain because she was no longer able to practice soothsaying. Her masters became angry due to her being freed from this possession and they sought to punish the Apostles by the city magistrate. We can conclude that all of the opposition to the church was prompted by Satan himself. All the hindrances, persecutions, and imprisonment were contrived by the devil. Satanic opposition to the church and to the churches scattered abroad, persecuted by mobs agitated by the priest and Jewish Pharisees, who were bitter because of the Apostles preaching about Jesus. Many of the priests were disturbed by the Deacon Stephen wisdom in his witness about Jesus, Acts 7:52-54. It tells of them "Gnashed on him with their teeth being better interpreted, "grounding their teeth in rage." This was the type of behavior of the Jewish leaders toward Stephen whom they subsequently stoned to death, which was capital punishment for blasphemy by Jewish law. All these types of activities were attributed to satanic opposition toward the church.

DEVILS ARE CAST OUT

In the 13th Chapter of the Book of Acts, the Apostle Paul came into confrontation with one Dlynas or sorcerer whom he accused of being "A child of the devil, thou enemy of all righteousness." The Apostle Paul condemned this person possessed by Satan and condemned him to blindness. The Apostle Paul on one missionary journey through the upper coast of Asia came to Ephesus and encountered some satanic activities, but in the disputes among priests, he was able to work miracles, by having handkerchiefs or aprons from his body applied to the sick and diseased. They were not only healed, but evil spirits went out of them. This caused Vagabond Jews to try to exorcise devils too, (cast them out). These trying to be exorcised were not ordained by Christ, who was called the "Sons of Sceva" tried to cast out devils who said to them "Jesus I know and Paul I know, but who are you?" These demons leaped on them, overcoming them in so much, that they fled out of the house naked and wounded, Acts 19:15,16.

Phillip, the Evangelist, did great works in the City of Samaria, causing unclean spirits, crying with a loud voice to come out of many possessed with evil spirits. Great joy came to this city that was under satanic dominations before the coming of Phillip, the Evangelist.

Once when Paul and Barnabas did great and mighty works in Iconium, Lystra, Derbe, and Lycaonia, the priest of these Greek cities wanted to do a sacrifice in honor of Paul and Barnabas, who were perplexed at the thought of these pagan worshippers looking upon them as gods, calling Paul and Barnabas by the Greek god names of Jupiter and Mercurius. The Apostles warned them and preached the true gospel to them that God who in times past suffered paganism, has now shown the true God through Jesus Christ, Acts 14:10-18.

APOSTOLIC LETTERS TO THE CHURCH CONCERNING SATAN

1. Pauline and the Apostle Epistles (letters)

The Apostle Paul uncovers for the church the schemes, methods, operations of Satan to the body of Christ. In the book entitled,

"Lest Satan Gets an Advantage of You," denotes that in the church's operation of doing God's work, Satan has many tricks called "Devices" that he seeks to undermine the people of God. The Apostle Paul in the letter to the Corinthian Church, Chapter 11 beginning at verse 14 says "And no marvel; For Satan himself is transformed into an angel of light (vs 15) says, therefore, it is no great thing if his ministers also be transformed as ministers of righteousness; whose end shall be according to their works." It is also translated in another version or a more modern tongue. "Oh, I'm not surprised that Satan can change himself into an angel of light so it's no wonder his servants can do it too." This knowledge of satanic activities and the guise of religion was noticed by Apostle Paul. He warns the Corinthian saints also that there are in the church under the cloak, those false apostles, deceitful workers, transforming themselves in the Apostle of Christ. This makes the ministry and the body of Christ think in terms of being on the alert. The Apostle John says in I John 4:1, "Beloved, believe not every spirit but try the spirits whether they are of God because many false prophets are gone out into the world." This also sets the stage for the resistance movements in the church against satanic activities, waged against the members in Christ's body. The Apostle Paul further warns the saints of the greater power and networks of satanic forces in the world in his letter to the Ephesians when he tells them "Put on the whole armor of God, that ye may be able to stand against the wiles of the devil," Ephesians 6:11. Also translated "Put on all of God's armor so you can be able to stand safe against all strategies and tricks of Satan." This plainly states to the saints that there are divine safeguards against Satan, such as stated by the Apostle James, 4:7, "Resist the devil and he will flee from you." The devil becomes powerless when the church uses the right types of armor in this resistance movement of satanic practices. Therefore, the different types of armors are spelled out in Ephesians 6, such as having your waist wrapped about with the truth, breastplate of righteousness to cover your heart with righteousness, put on the shoes of the gospel having your feet shod with the preparation of the gospel of peace. That is the peace that God makes with all men through the good news of Jesus Christ. Put on your head, the helmet of Salvation and the sword of the spirit, which is the Word of God. One of the greatest pieces of armor or weapons of warfare against Satan is lastly stated, "The sword of the Spirit" which is the Word of God, which is the devil's nightmare, the instrument that destroys his works. Jesus told Satan in the Gospel of Luke, Chapter 4, "Man shall not live by bread alone, but by every word that proceeded out of the mouth of God." The word gives life to every believer and Jesus himself defeated every trial of Satan by saying, "It is written" thus establishing the trend for our spiritual warfare against satanic attacks that is by His Word, and His Word alone. The Apostles warnings to the early church concerning Satan and his activities is spelled out in Romans 1:28, "And even as they did not like to retain God in their knowledge, God gave them over to a reprobate mind to do those things which are not convenient," or better translated, "God gave them up to doing every evil thing their mind could think of." Satan fulfilling his desire, to trick the minds of men so they would not be able to distinguish wrong from right, God from Satan, Holiness from sin, thus causing extreme consequences upon the human race. It is written also in Romans, Chapter 1 verse 18, The wrath or anger" of God is revealed from heaven against all ungodliness and unrighteousness of men who hold the truth in unrighteousness, having a preacher to preach to them and they still do things contrary to the law and purpose of God, will not as the Apostle Paul says, Have No Excuse." Therefore, the Apostles come out in their letters to the churches in support of the scriptures that Satan does come against the church as the Apostle John states in, I John 5:19 "And we know what we are of God, and the whole world lieth in wickedness." The Apostle John also states that he who sinned is of the Devil, because of the Devil sinneth from the beginning, I John 3:8. Paul, Peter and the Apostle John wrote epistles to the churches that were scattered, persecuted, and struggling to make the gospel message of Jesus Christ known to the Roman Empire and its providence. It was the Apostle Paul who stated, "For we wrestle not against flesh and blood but against principalities and against powers, against the rules of the darkness of this world, against spiritual wickedness in high places." Though Satan came against the church in the form of hostile government laws, and the Jewish hierarchy that did not want Christianity to spread in the providences where Jews were subject to the Romans, being allowed to continue Judaism. However, Paul states that behind the whole scheme of things its due to "Principalities, Powers, and works of darkness, the powers without bodies - the evil rulers of the unseen world, Ephesians 6:12. Thus, we conclude that the epistles, as letters, inspired by God inform us of the assaults upon the body of Christ comes directly from Satan himself. The Apostle Paul did warn the saints not to let Satan get an advantage over you - for "We are not ignorant of his devices."

Satanic Activities During Apostolic Times

Summary

After the outpouring of the Holy Ghost in the early church, the Apostles were able to apply their power over demons, as they met them during the infancy of the church. The same power that Jesus bestowed upon the Apostles in Luke 10:19, "I give you power over all the power of the enemy and nothing shall hurt you." If the church was to suffer from violence, then the church has the power to "fight back" not the carnal fight of physical weapons, but to fight the spiritual warfare, the good fight of faith. The church has the promise to be the ultimate victor, and the gates of hell would not overcome it. As the church ventured out into the Roman providences, and other areas of the gentile world, the battle against Satan became more and more acute and fierce. Thus, the Jewish faith, the Pharisees practicing Judaism, and the pagan idolatry, were enemies to Christ. Satan would stir up the groups to fight the newly founded Christian church. The church stood the test and "fought back" against the spiritual wickedness by "casting out devils in the name of Jesus." Although Satan operates under the veil of a religious disguise in opposing the church, the apostles were wise and full of spiritual knowledge and wisdom, seeing the plan of Satan in both the Jewish and Pagan gentile opposition. The Apostle Paul even knew of those within the Christian church, who did not see his total vision of Christ for the church and he often uttered the words of "Fears from without and doubts from within." Thus, he would write concerning those who preached Christ of envy and strife, some preaching, trying to add affliction to his bonds and of perils among false brethren, Phil. 1:15,16. All of these oppositions against the body of Christ, which was the early church, the church of the Apostles, were due directly from Satanic attacks in one form or another. The Bible talks of the triumph of the persecuted church in the book of the Revelation of Jesus Christ. Both the church of yesterday and the church of today have the victory over the devil by the blood of Jesus and the power of his might. Therefore, the writings and the letters to the church gave instructions, warnings, and positive assurances, that the church will become "More than Conquerors" through the Power of Christ.

CHAPTER 5

THE CHURCH OF GOD IN CHRIST'S POSITION ON SATANISM

We, in the Church of God in Christ believe as many Christian Churches who embrace the Judeo-Christian's philosophy about such subjects as the rejection of idolatry, wizardry, and pagan superstitions perpetrated by Satan. Concerning the Mosaic denouncement of such, he was quoted as saying in Mt. 5:17, "Think not that I have come to destroy the law or the prophets: I am come to fulfill." Therefore, Moses commands to put to death those with "familiar spirits, who practice sorcery, or witches that practice witchcraft, Ex. 22:18; I Sam. 28:9. These did represent the gods of Egypt and idolatry. Though we do not look upon these practices as worthy of capital punishment, adhering to the civil law which recognizes these as entertainment, we do denounce them as evil spiritual practices, not to be observed by Christian saints. In our Official Manual of the Church of God in Christ, pages 50-51, we address the topic of "Demonology." We believe in the Apostle Paul's doctrine concerning demonic practices, evil principalities, and workers of evil in this present world. Ephesians 6:12. We believe they can be overcome, defeated, and cast out. The Church of God in Christ believes that the modem Holy Ghost filled saint has the power to cast out devils by the authority in the name of Jesus. Mk. 16:17. We further believe in the teaching of the Apostles such as James, which admonishes us to "Resist the devil and he will flee from you," James 4:7. We also believe that the teaching of Jesus indicates that some illnesses and afflictions are caused by devils, such was the case in Mk. 9:29, when Jesus admonishes the disciples who could not heal the boy with the dumb spirit and Jesus replied, Some of these come forth only, but by prayer and fasting. Thus, setting forth the spiritual discipline of consecration through fasting and praying to cast out satanic powers in the Church of God in Christ. We are accustomed to hearing the prayers and commands of Bishop C. H. Mason, our founder, who said, "Satan the Lord Rebuke Thee." We believe what the Apostle Paul taught in Ephesians 6:12, that the devil is an invisible force, not flesh and blood. That he is powerful and controls spiritual darkness and is the ruler of spiritual wickedness in this world. However, saints have many protective armors to combat his spiritual powers. He says, "We are more than conquerors," Romans 8:37. We, in the Church of God in Christ, also believe that devils, satanic practices, are in many deceptive forms, and appear to be of help to individuals seeking betterment and fulfillment, such as; fortune-telling, and mediums who seek to communicate with dead loved ones, sorcerers, witches, mediums, and wizards. We do believe in the Prophet Isaiah's denunciation of the multitude of counsels of Astrologers (star readers), stargazers, the monthly prognosticators (horoscope readers), etc. We must take the position as Spirit-filled saints that nothing outside of God can be of help to us, not luck, good or bad, not soothsaying or any other type of magic or black arts. We believe they are of the devil. Saints do not believe in "luck" we believe in blessings. We do not play the "Lottery," church gambling is an evil practice for saints; and those who engage in gambling are those in the environment of corrupt, evil persons. The Bible says "evil communication corrupts good manners," I Cor. 15:33. God is our source, not "chance or gambling," these are evil satanic devices. "But godliness with contentment is great gain. For we brought nothing into this world, and we can certainly carry nothing out. "And having food and raiment Let us be therewith content but they that will be rich fall into temptation and a snare, and into many foolish and hurtful lusts, which drown men in destruction and perdition. For the love of money is the root of all evil: which while some coveted after, they have erred from the faith, and pierced themselves through with many sorrows," I Timothy 6:6-10.

Now, we must touch upon a crucial, and critical subject that may offend many so-called "Saints" or Christians, and those of "Secret Order Societies," Secret Lodges, or Secret Sororities, etc. In the Church of God in Christ, our founding father, Bishop C. H. Mason, preached against and denounced "Secret Orders" and "Secret Lodges" which he condemns as being of the devil. Ironically, some secret orders do propose to be Christian. They require church membership before qualifying for membership. As one author puts it, the type of Christianity they promulgate is "Blasphemy."

According to the author, William Schnoebelen, who wrote the book entitled, "Masonry Beyond the Light," when one enters the secret lodge he/she will take a solemn oath, secret handshakes and secret words of the lodge that are passed on to him and the secret, sacred name of God. That true name of God is this so-called Christian, God respecting Lodge is JAHBULON. But when one breaks down its roots, we find it steeped in old paganism, JAH, which is not bad, means JEHOVAH. The second syllable, BUL means BEL of BAAL the evil god of Jezebel and Ahab, and the last syllable of ON or "Orin." The pagan god of the "Sun."

Abraham was commanded by God to get out of his father's house, his country, and his kindred because those of Mesopotamia were worshippers of nature gods such as the "Sun-god." This secret name, JAHBULON, is an "Unholy Trinity" carved out of evil satanic paganism, that offers to any Christian no spiritual enrichment, certainly none outside of the church; the only Christian assembly that is supposed to teach the open, not "secret" Word of God. The secret lodges, styles Jesus Christ as the "Great Architect" not the loving Savior, the Son of the Almighty God, the Creator of the universe. He was more than the mere "carpenter" that secret lodges try to box him in. In the secret lodge, says Mr. Schnoebelen, Jesus is not looked upon as the Christ, the Savior of the world, but rather the so-called limited GHETTO JESUS or a Jesus squeezed into the mold of the cosmetic Jesus, who required one to be saved through some penitence. Those desiring membership to the many satanically controlled secret lodges, reciting the many oaths that are not biblical. Many fruitless hours are spent in these secret lodges, which attempt to take the place of the church. Jesus never intended that secret lodges be part or an assistant to, helping the ministry of the church which he said he would build, and the gates of Hell should not prevail against it. We join with Bishop C. H. Mason in denouncing secret lodges as "dens of iniquities, sepulchers of evil men."

Therefore, we conclude that the church of God in Christ considers all these evil satanic devices to be of the devil. We are admonished not to drink of the cup of the Lord and the cup of the devil, and ye cannot be partakers of the Lord's table, and of the table of devils, which has more significance than just the Lord's supper and communion. One cannot be partakers of satanic practices in the move of Christ and the Christian church. The Apostle Paul admonishes the church, We are not ignorant of satanic devices, which we believe are the many so-called bits of help that are super-spiritual agents of mysticism, ancient black arts, horoscopes, mediums, etc. The secret lodges that offer a closer walk with God, but are deceptive devices that confuse un-watchful Christians and the innocent seekers of God and Truth.

WHY DON'T WE BELIEVE ISLAM?

The Church of God in Christ, which is a Pentecostal "Holiness Faith" that embraces both the Judeo-Christian heritage in the Protestant persuasion, being fully Christian in our devotion and adhering to the scriptures. "This is my Beloved Son, whom I am well pleased," Luke 3:32. Wherefore, God also hath highly exalted Him and given him a name which is above "every name," that at the name of Jesus every knee should bow of things in heaven and things in earth, and things under the earth; and that every tongue shall confess that Jesus Christ is Lord, to the Glory of God, the Father," Philippians 2:9,10. In these two passages of scripture it definitely does not give any room for the favoring or recognizing or taking serious notice to any man, not even the great patriarch, prophets, kings, priests, and certainly not to a religion called "Islam" whose god is called "Allah," whose person is called "Muhammad and whose Bible is called the "The Holy Koran."

Muhammad, founder of Islam, who according to history was born in Mecca in 570 A.D., son of a desert nomad. He was supposedly to belong to a Caravan Tribe of notorious robbers that pilgrimage other tribes and engaged in Slave Trade. Being true to the scripture reference of Ishmael, "he will be a wild man his hand against every man, and every man's hand against him and he shall dwell in the presence of all his brethren. Ishmael is the father of all Arabs and Muslims Muhammad being an Arab and dwelt among his hated-half-brother, the Jew. After Muhammad's mother and father passed away, according to the historical record of one Prof. Peter a Michas, he was raised by his uncle, Abvtalib, and his cousin, Ali. His uncle, his cousin, and his children founded Islam. After some time, Muhammad was supposed to hear voices and see visions and chose the pagan god. "Allah" as the one to worship. This new-found religion, that set out to conquer the world through military expeditions and conquests of the "Holy War," the "JIHAD." All who are not Muslim, are regarded as infidels must be either brought under subjection or destroyed. After conquering Mecca and expelling all Christians and Jews, he proclaimed the sole deity of "Allah" denouncing all plurality of gods even the Trinity. The Islamic Terms Peace (Salaam) means also to submit, and world peace is the complete domination of all infidels and to rule and govern all under the "Sharia" or Islam's Barbaric Common Law.

Muhammad versus Christianity although the Muslim faith adopts Abraham as one of its patriarch fathers, declares Jesus as a (minor) prophet of Allah. The Moslem's Holy Koran does mention Moses, David, Isaac, and Ishmael as the promised child, not Isaac.

Although Islam seeks to stamp out all other forms of religion, even other pagan religions, it does not accept the co-existence of Judaism and Christianity, which in future conquests seeks to eliminate by all means, even by military conquest. Therefore, the Islamic religion does not accept Jesus Christ as Son of God, as the Savior of the world, or as the Messiah to this earth to save all men. The true Arabian Moslem, embracing the Muslim faith of Islam, has not changed in this modern twentieth century, but is rather still bent on military conquest, to expel all infidels in their violent creed; to create a militant power, to overthrow all governments and persons not under the Moslem faith of Islam.

Therefore, we conclude as Christians of the faith of our Lord Jesus Christ, that Mugwump as a man, not a God, must stand before the Judgement Seat of Jesus, to be judged. Whose name is not in the Lambs Book of Life, and if his name is in the book of Islam called "Koran" then God will not accept him, falling short of the required judgment of God. Paul asserted to the Athenian Greeks on Mars Hill, "That God had appointed a day in which he will judge the world in righteousness by the man (Christ Jesus) whom he hath ordained," Acts 17:33.

THE NEW AGE MOVEMENT

"The Worship of Another god"

The end of the 20th Century and the approach of the 21st Century will bring more increasing evidence of subtle satanic practices and activities in the world. Jesus said in Matthew 24:24 "For there shall arise false Christ's (deceivers) and false prophets (preachers), and shall shew great signs and wonders." This being the case for this generation, one certainly must be alert to the many signs and wonders of this new age, that will practice the old witchcraft and sorcery in a different mask. We know of the increasing attention paid to the Zodiac signs, horoscopes, and the positive thinking methods that exclude God. In the Western world, much attention is given to Eastern mysticism and occultism. Much of these newer trends come from the conditioning of "humanism" which teaches the supreme authority of man's ability to determine his own goals, and destiny, without the authority of the scriptures of God. The mystic Gurus of the East find this generation, high on drugs and intoxicated with a new rebellion, easy prey to the new philosophies, that are truly anti-Judeo-Christian. The ultimate goal of the teaching of the New Age Movement is to destroy beliefs in patriotism, traditional moral values of the church. The New-Age Movement crept into the Christian community because of religious apathy, disillusionment, disappointments, and hypocrisy. Much of these newer satanic principles taught to this generation is a challenge like that to Eve spoken by the serpent (Satan). "Thou shalt not surely die," Genesis 3:4. Among some of the new world order; will be that of "self-definition" (man is god) and reincarnation, which teaches that one may die and re-appear in different forms of plant, animal, or other. These two are clearly from the Eastern cult teachings; which primarily comes from India. The teaching of pantheism, which makes God impersonal and an illusory matter that inhabits all forms. It also has some of the humanistic, teaching that man is the supreme creature and the god of this earth. The method of falling into trances in the Transcendental meditations ritual will cause the man to separate, the spirit from the body; thus, liberating man from the mundane trends bringing about some sense of salvation. The New Age Movement has a whole different moral concept of "right and wrong," "good and bad." These teachings are anti-Christian and anti-biblical. This new teaching or "enlightenment" comes to rid one of the ignorance thus erasing sin or wrong. If one engages in the lower values of wrong and sins, it's because he has not accepted the ritual of "enlightenment that usually results from some method of successive Chants and Trances." You may have seen the "Hare Krishna" in their meditation chants on the street. Many of our servicemen also encountered many of these Eastern religious practices and brought them back to the States.

The New Age Movement does creep into the American Society and eventually the Christian community due to the seemingly harmless belief in horoscopes and astronomy. We are supposedly living in the Age of the "Aquarius," The Water-Age, along with the physical preparation of "Yoga." Many of these have been introduced as afore stated by the "godmen" of the East, the "Gurus" and the "Bhagwans." These men claim to have supernatural power, much coming from their physical trances of "Yoga." This Hindu practice of "Yoga" which means "Yoke" is meant to unite man with Brahmanism, which represents the "god of everything." He is the god of both good and bad and is the supreme god of the universe. This practice of "Yoga" will usher one into the newer alternatives of ideals dealing with "peace," "love," "integrity," and "salvation." All these, of course, are anti-Christian but ripe for an age that has lost faith in God and the church. This generation, seduced by the Devil, is looking for another alternative to the Christian church and the Bible. Eager to try anything new such as "biofeedback," hypnosis and of course psychedelic music, devilish music, especially designed for the "rock," "pop" age. Self-realization and positive imaging, which is not bad within itself (learning to love one's self), but when one embarks upon these goals of life, he is immediately introduced to a new-god to worship, a new creed to obey, a new Bible to read and follow; thus, ushering in a new age concept to the individual.

The New Age programs that are already invading the

American community are devilish, cunning, rebellious, and ungodly. As fore stated they are the old paganistic, heathenistic practices in newer forms, newer practices, such as "Transcendental meditation," which offers a new hypnotic high, to those who are apt to follow through the harmless adherence to the zodiac and horoscope signs that appear in our everyday newspapers. Finally, one must adhere to the warning of the Apostles concerning these "last days" that there would be those giving "Heed to doctrines of devils and seducing spirits," I Tim. 4:1. And of course, one in the church can see that the New Age Movement, with its doctrines and practices, are demonic in their inception. They tend to lead one away from the faith, from the God of Abraham, Isaac, and Jacob, and of course, they are against the teachings of Jesus Christ, the Son of the Living God. Eastern cults have found fertile soil in the Western culture due to apathy a rebellion of the youth and the desire to try a new god, which is the god of the New age, which is still the devil in different garments.

CHAPTER 6

THE POWER OF THE TONGUE OVER SATAN

THE DEVIL IS ACTIVE AND effective, but God has not left his people defenseless. God has left the believers the weapons of His Word to attack the enemy and defeat him. We only have to be knowledgeable of our Lord and how He dealt with Satan in the wilderness when the devil came against him to tempt him. Jesus used the Word of God for the New Testament was not written. Jesus quoted from Deuteronomy 8:3(b), "That he might make thee know that man doth not live by bread only, but by every word that proceedeth out of the mouth of the Lord doth man live."

In the devil's second assault, Jesus quoted Deuteronomy 6:16, "Ye shall not tempt the Lord your God, as ye tempted him in Massah;" and when the devil came against him the third time, Jesus quoted Deuteronomy 10:20; "Thou shalt fear the Lord thy God: him shalt thou serve, and to him shalt thou cleave, and swear by his name." Each time the devil came against him, Jesus used the Word of God against Satan and successfully defeated him.

Matthew 4:11, "Then the devil leaveth him and behold Angels came and ministered unto him." When we use the weapon of God's word, the devil in Hell cannot withstand us. God sent the Angels to minister to Jesus, the Holy Ghost comes to help our infirmities (weaknesses), Romans 8:26.

When Jesus spoke to the demons in Legion, He took authority over them by commanding them and telling them where to go, Mark 5:8-14. The demons knew they were subject to Jesus, so they asked permission of Jesus to go into the swine and did not move until Jesus gave them permission, Mark 5:11-13.

Before one can be saved, one must speak it with one's mouth. To be baptized with the Holy Ghost, one must claim it, therefore as believers in Christ and empowered by God (Acts 1:8). We have the authority to speak and command the devil and his imps as did Michael the Archangel in Jude 1:9(b).

God gives the believer the Power of the Tongue to speak to the enemy or mountain in his/her life, Proverbs 18:21. "Death and life are in the power of the tongue and they that love it shall eat the fruit thereof." A man that speaks negatively to his wife and belittles her can destroy her confidence and self-esteem and vice versa: Parents who belittle their children or even think negatively of themselves lose their self-esteem and ultimately become a loser and disappointed with themselves and with life.

It was Jesus who told the disciples that they could speak to the mountain (sickness, financial difficulties, domestic problems, etc.), and order it to be moved out of the way and command it where to go, and believe in his heart that those things which he SAITH, shall come to pass. He shall have whatever he SAITH, Mark 11:23.

I had a young man who had been to several exorcists to have the devil cast out of him because he was hearing voices that instructed him to do various evil deeds that he knew were wrong and caused him to use foul language. The exorcism was unsuccessful, he was unable to eat, and hadn't slept in three days because of the voices. We prayed and spoke to those demons that were tormenting him and commanded them to leave, anointing him with oil in the name of Jesus, according to James 5:14. I instructed him to read Mark 11:23,24, as well as Jude 1:9(b) and told him to speak to those voices and command them in the name of Jesus, rebuking them with the authority invested in him as a believer.

The brother came back to me a few days later praising God because he was no longer hearing the voices, he was sleeping all night and eating once again. The power to speak to your mountain is your authority from God. One must have confidence in what one speaks in the name of Jesus (the authority of Christ), but believe the things which you speak, and they shall come to pass. He shall have whatever he SAITH, Mark 11:23(b). And this is the confidence that we have in him that if we ask anything according to His will, He heareth us and if we know' that He heareth us, we have the assurance that we can have what we have petitioned, I John 5:13,14.

Jesus had so much confidence in His power and what He spoke that he stood at the grave of Lazarus and before He prayed, He cried out, **"Father I thank thee that thou hast heard me, And I know that Thou hearest me always."** St. John 11:41(b), 42(a).

As ambassadors for Christ and being in Christ's stead, Jesus has given us the Power of Attorney to use his name. Anything we ask in His name that will He do; So, the Father may be glorified in the Son and that Christ may be glorified in us. No matter what the situation, don't maximize the problem and minimize God; Ask, Believe, and Receive!

THE FINAL SUMMARY

In the book "Overcoming Satanic Devices" I have endeavored to show in this modern church age of which the Church of God In Christ is a part, that Satana is still at work with his many schemes and methods. We have shown in the beginning as early as Pre-Abrahamic times, the heathenistic practices of the devil in the many forms of false gods, idol worship, and many other paganistic practices. The Muslim faith of "Allah" god had its roots in these early paganistic practices adopted by Mugwump himself. In the early history of America after World War I, Elijah Mugwump adopted his brand of the Muslim faith, seeking to give Blacks an alternative religion opposite of his white racist brethren, who were Christians. We have shown that both Israel and the Christian church encountered satanic practices in some form or another. Even the prophet Isaiah warned backsliding Israel that their many psychiatric counselors, stargazers, monthly prognosticators, would not be able to help them from the coming judgment, Isaiah 47:14.

In the New Testament, Jesus was able to separate satanic oppression in affliction and sickness. He healed many and cast the devil out. The Apostles encountered Satanism especially among the Gentiles, under the yoke of heathens. The New Age concepts are still those of many evils that appear harmless but are subtle efforts of Satan to infiltrate the Christian church and the teachings of Christ. The Church of God in Christ must be alert to the many faces and mask of Satan and in keeping with our founder, Bishop C. H. Mason, who was in opposition to the devil, even as the Angel Michael who said, "Satan the Lord rebuke thee," Jude 1:9.

We must conclude that this book was dedicated to the Christians, the Saints, who are to be on guard against all the works of Satan, and as the Apostle, Paul stated, "We are not ignorant of his devices," that may be in operation and practice in this present world.

Bishop & Mrs. Nathaniel W. Wells, Jr.

To Re-Order, Write to:

Holy Trinity Church
P.O. Box 4497
Muskegon Heights, Michigan 4944

www.ingramcontent.com/pod-product-compliance
Lightning Source LLC
LaVergne TN
LVHW020438080526
838202LV00055B/5244